Martyn Payne

C000005689

The Easter Story

for families to share

readings, questions, activities and prayers

1 Jesus arrives in Jerusalem

²⁸ After Jesus had said this, he went on ahead, going up to Jerusalem. ²⁹ As he approached Bethphage and Bethany at the hill called the Mount of Olives, he sent two of his disciples, saying to them, ³⁰ 'Go to the village ahead of you, and as you enter it, you will find a colt tied there, which no one has ever ridden. Untie it and bring it here. ³¹ If anyone asks you, "Why are you untying it?" say, "The Lord needs it."'

³² Those who were sent ahead went and found it just as he had told them. ³³ As they were untying the colt, its owners asked them, 'Why are you untying the colt?'

³⁴ They replied, 'The Lord needs it.'

³⁵ They brought it to Jesus, threw their cloaks on the colt and put Jesus on it. ³⁶ As he went along, people spread their cloaks on the road.

³⁷ When he came near the place where the road goes down the Mount of Olives, the whole crowd of disciples began joyfully to praise God in loud voices for all the miracles they had seen:

³⁸ 'Blessed is the king who comes in the name of the Lord!'
'Peace in heaven and glory in the highest!'

³⁹ Some of the Pharisees in the crowd said to Jesus, 'Teacher, rebuke your disciples!'

⁴⁰ 'I tell you,' he replied, 'if they keep quiet, the stones will cry out.'

LUKE 19:28–40

Commentary

The final week of Jesus' life arrives. It is such an important week that each of the gospels devotes several chapters to the events of the next few days. The news of Jesus' wonderful deeds, teaching and healing people, assures him of a hero's welcome into Jerusalem on the day we now call Palm Sunday.

In the style of a victory procession for a Roman general, people line the streets, waving palms and throwing their clothes on to the road to make a sort of red carpet for a new king. They shout out an extravagant welcome, believing that Jesus has come to rescue them from the Romans. Their words about peace and glory are almost an echo of what the angels sang on the night Jesus was born, but, just as the arrival of the king then as a helpless baby was unexpected, so this arrival takes everyone by surprise too. He chooses to ride a donkey, not a fine white stallion, which would have better suited a great king. Jesus is a different sort of king; even so, he recognises that this is a day of rejoicing because an amazing rescue is about to happen, one that the crowds cannot begin to imagine.

?? Questions

▶ What makes you think that Jesus had planned ahead for this special day?

▶ What was so special about this particular donkey?

▶ Why had such large crowds gathered to welcome Jesus?

▶ What sort of king was everyone expecting?

▶ Why were the Pharisees so upset?

Visual aid

Find a branch with large leaves to be your 'palms' for this story. You might even be able to find a real palm leaf somewhere, or perhaps a cross made from palm leaves.

 # Activity idea

Many Christians receive a palm cross at church on the Sunday when we remember this story. You may already have one. On the internet there are instructions for how to fold paper to make your own palm cross. Once you have something to wave, recreate the sounds of that day, cheering and shouting 'Hosanna!', which means 'Save us!'

 # Prayer idea

Use the palms of your hands to signpost different sorts of prayer.

- Wave the palms of your hands in praise of Jesus.
- Hold up your palms asking Jesus to be king of your life this day.
- Turn over your palms to let go of all that is bad.
- Press together the palms of your hands and ask God to help you to be ready to say 'yes'.
- Stretch out your palms to bless each other in the name of the one who comes in the name of the Lord.

Old Testament story link

Long ago, the prophet Zechariah wrote about the way in which the special king from God would arrive in Jerusalem.
ZECHARIAH 9:9–10

Key verse
'Blessed is the king who comes in the name of the Lord!'
LUKE 19:38

2 Cleansing the temple

¹³ When it was almost time for the Jewish Passover, Jesus went up to Jerusalem. ¹⁴ In the temple courts he found people selling cattle, sheep and doves, and others sitting at tables exchanging money. ¹⁵ So he made a whip out of cords, and drove all from the temple courts, both sheep and cattle; he scattered the coins of the money-changers and overturned their tables. ¹⁶ To those who sold doves he said, 'Get these out of here! Stop turning my Father's house into a market!' ¹⁷ His disciples remembered that it is written: 'Zeal for your house will consume me.'

¹⁸ The Jews then responded to him, 'What sign can you show us to prove your authority to do all this?'

¹⁹ Jesus answered them, 'Destroy this temple, and I will raise it again in three days.'

²⁰ They replied, 'It has taken forty-six years to build this temple, and you are going to raise it in three days?' ²¹ But the temple he had spoken of was his body. ²² After he was raised from the dead, his disciples recalled what he had said. Then they believed the Scripture and the words that Jesus had spoken.

JOHN 2:13–22

💬 Commentary

To worship at the temple in Jerusalem for one of the great festivals was a high point for any Jewish believer. This was particularly true of the annual Passover celebrations, which commemorated the time when God rescued the nation from being slaves in Egypt. Thousands of pilgrims arrived and crowded into the outer courts, eager to buy the necessary animals – mainly sheep or doves – to use in the special ceremonies. The religious leaders set up market stalls and also, because the use of Roman coins was forbidden in the temple precincts, a place to change money into the right currency to spend. In fact, it had become a huge money-making event – that is, until Jesus appeared.

When he visited the temple as a young boy, Jesus told Mary that this was his Father's house, and it is these words that echo around the building again as he drives out all those who are buying and selling. When challenged by the authorities, he replies with what seems to them to be a riddle, claiming that, should the temple be destroyed, he will rebuild it in three days. Only much later did his disciples realise what he had been saying. He was predicting his resurrection; however, the Jewish leaders took his words literally and stored them up as evidence to use against him when they put him on trial for insulting the temple and their God.

⁇ Questions

▶ Does it surprise you that Jesus acted so violently in this story?

▶ What was it exactly that made Jesus so angry?

▶ What did Jesus mean about rebuilding the temple in three days?

▶ When, if ever, is it right to be really angry like this?

Visual aid

Turn a small table upside down and use it as a focus for today's story. Jesus was always turning ideas upside down, and now even the furniture is being overturned!

 # Activity idea

This is a story of great noise and confusion. Divide up the following sound effects among you as a family: the bleating of sheep, the lowing of cattle, the cooing of doves, the rattle of coins falling, the shouts of the stallholders and the angry voice of Jesus. Rehearse the sounds individually and then, on the count of three, all join together to recreate the noise in the temple on the day Jesus arrived. Make Jesus' words the last and loudest sound to be heard.

 # Prayer idea

For each of the different things in the story, create a prayer that asks God to help you not to make the same mistakes – for example, 'May we not be like sheep and wander from you'; 'May we not be like foolish cattle and miss hearing your voice'; 'May we be like doves, always knowing how to fly back home to you'; 'May we not be like coins spent on things that take us away from you.'

 # Old Testament story link

Hosea warns God's people of the dangers of falling away from him, but also predicts God's willingness to put them right again.
HOSEA 6:1–6

Key verse

Jesus answered them, 'Destroy this temple, and I will raise it again in three days.'
JOHN 2:19

3 The plot to kill Jesus

[1] Now the Festival of Unleavened Bread, called the Passover, was approaching, [2] and the chief priests and the teachers of the law were looking for some way to get rid of Jesus, for they were afraid of the people. [3] Then Satan entered Judas, called Iscariot, one of the Twelve. [4] And Judas went to the chief priests and the officers of the temple guard and discussed with them how he might betray Jesus. [5] They were delighted and agreed to give him money. [6] He consented, and watched for an opportunity to hand Jesus over to them when no crowd was present.

[7] Then came the day of Unleavened Bread on which the Passover lamb had to be sacrificed. [8] Jesus sent Peter and John, saying, 'Go and make preparations for us to eat the Passover.'

[9] 'Where do you want us to prepare for it?' they asked.

[10] He replied, 'As you enter the city, a man carrying a jar of water will meet you. Follow him to the house that he enters, [11] and say to the owner of the house, "The Teacher asks: where is the guest room, where I may eat the Passover with my disciples?" [12] He will show you a large room upstairs, all furnished. Make preparations there.'

[13] They left and found things just as Jesus had told them. So they prepared the Passover.

LUKE 22:1–13

Commentary

The storm clouds were gathering. Jesus' behaviour in the temple had dismayed many people and convinced the religious leaders that Jesus was becoming an embarrassment to them and a risk, because his behaviour could provoke the Roman soldiers to come down heavily on the festival crowds. They were also fearful of losing their own position of influence and power. They could see no other solution than to have Jesus killed.

It is hard to understand what Judas' motives were in striking a deal with the chief priests. Clearly money was involved. Perhaps he also thought that Jesus needed to confront the leaders and do a spectacular miracle to convince them that he was the true king. There is no doubt what the other disciples thought about him: he was a traitor in the grip of the devil.

In the meantime, it was clear that the one person really in charge was Jesus, who had arranged a place for them all to celebrate the special Passover meal. All they had to do was to follow a man with a water jar, which would have been an unusual sight in those days, and therefore came as an almost comical game of 'follow the leader' in what was otherwise such a tragic week.

Questions

▶ Why were the chief priests and teachers of the Law so eager to get rid of Jesus?

▶ Why do you think Judas struck a deal with the religious leaders?

▶ What makes you think Jesus had planned ahead?

▶ Who would you invite to a special meal for an important festival like the Passover?

Visual aid

Dress someone from the family in dark glasses and a hoodie with the hood up. This story is all about holding secret meetings, plotting and being on the lookout, like spies, for a particular sign that will lead you to the right place to be.

Activity idea

Try to work out what prompted Judas to go and meet the religious leaders. Divide into two groups and put Judas on trial, one group accusing him and the other trying to defend him. Work out what each of you thinks about Judas and also consider what Jesus would have thought about him. Do you think Jesus would have understood and forgiven him?

Prayer idea

Whatever we think about Judas, he stands as a warning to each of us not to do the wrong thing. We all need help to discover the way ahead when faced by hard decisions. Use the letters of the name JUDAS to help you pray about this. For example, ask God to help you to **Judge** tricky situations properly; **Understand** the way to go; **Decide** what will be good for other people, not just yourself; **Admit** your need; and **Seek** God's will.

Old Testament story link

Here is a psalm of David with advice about making the right choices in life.
PSALM 37:1–9

Key verse
They left and found things just as Jesus had told them.
LUKE 22:13

4 The last supper

¹⁴ When the hour came, Jesus and his apostles reclined at the table.
¹⁵ And he said to them, 'I have eagerly desired to eat this Passover with you before I suffer. ¹⁶ For I tell you, I will not eat it again until it finds fulfilment in the kingdom of God.'

¹⁷ After taking the cup, he gave thanks and said, 'Take this and divide it among you. ¹⁸ For I tell you I will not drink again from the fruit of the vine until the kingdom of God comes.'

¹⁹ And he took bread, gave thanks and broke it, and gave it to them, saying, 'This is my body given for you; do this in remembrance of me.'

²⁰ In the same way, after the supper he took the cup, saying, 'This cup is the new covenant in my blood, which is poured out for you. ²¹ But the hand of him who is going to betray me is with mine on the table. ²² The Son of Man will go as it has been decreed. But woe to that man who betrays him!' ²³ They began to question among themselves which of them it might be who would do this.

LUKE 22:14–23

Commentary

The Passover meal is still celebrated every year in Jewish homes. There are particular words that are said and certain foods eaten, which help tell the story of how God rescued the Hebrews from slavery in Egypt. Each cup of wine has special prayers linked to it, and the bread is flat because it is made without yeast. The first Passover meal was eaten in such a rush that there was no time to wait for the dough to rise. At this meal, they remember how the angel of death had passed over the Israelites' homes, which had been marked with lamb's blood on the doorposts. It was therefore not just an escape from slavery but from death itself.

Jesus was the host for this particular Passover meal with his friends, but, to their surprise, he took some of the traditional parts of the ceremony and gave them new meanings. He described the bread as his body and the wine as his blood. He wanted his disciples to have a way of remembering his death, now only hours away, which would rescue them just as the blood on the doorposts had saved the Israelites long ago. It was the only way Jesus could rescue the world and already, because of Judas, plans for his capture, trial and crucifixion were well under way.

?? Questions

▶ Can you imagine what the atmosphere was like during this Passover meal?

▶ Why do Christians today call this 'the last supper'?

▶ What good news does Jesus share at this meal before he begins talking about his body and blood?

▶ Have you ever been to a church service where this meal has been re-enacted? What happened?

Visual aid

You will need a piece of bread that has been made without yeast (for example, Matzo) and a cup of juice or non-alcoholic wine. Jesus gave these ordinary items of food and drink special meanings at the last supper.

 # Activity idea

Find out what is eaten at a typical Jewish Passover meal. You could research this as a family from a book or on the internet. How is each item of food at the meal linked to the story of the escape from Egypt?

 # Prayer idea

Eating the bread and drinking the wine are ways of remembering Jesus and what happened on Good Friday. Talk about the special reminders you could carry with you to help you remember to pray for your family, your friends, people in need and people far away. For example, you could choose ribbons of different colours, or beads that are differently shaped. Decide what you as a family will use as reminders while you are away from each other and from home.

 # Old Testament story link

Moses gives instructions about the bread to be used at the Passover meal.
EXODUS 13:3–10

Key verse
Jesus… broke it, and gave it to them, saying, 'This is my body.'
LUKE 22:19

5 Gethsemane

[36] Then Jesus went with his disciples to a place called Gethsemane, and he said to them, 'Sit here while I go over there and pray.' [37] He took Peter and the two sons of Zebedee along with him, and he began to be sorrowful and troubled. [38] Then he said to them, 'My soul is overwhelmed with sorrow to the point of death. Stay here and keep watch with me.'

[39] Going a little farther, he fell with his face to the ground and prayed, 'My Father, if it is possible, may this cup be taken from me. Yet not as I will, but as you will.'

[40] Then he returned to his disciples and found them sleeping. 'Couldn't you men keep watch with me for one hour?' he asked Peter. [41] 'Watch and pray so that you will not fall into temptation. The spirit is willing, but the flesh is weak.'

[42] He went away a second time and prayed, 'My Father, if it is not possible for this cup to be taken away unless I drink it, may your will be done.'

[43] When he came back, he again found them sleeping, because their eyes were heavy. [44] So he left them and went away once more and prayed the third time, saying the same thing.

[45] Then he returned to the disciples and said to them, 'Are you still sleeping and resting? Look, the hour has come, and the Son of Man is delivered into the hands of sinners. [46] Rise! Let us go! Here comes my betrayer!'

MATTHEW 26:36-46

💬 Commentary

At Gethsemane there was a garden of olive trees, which seems to have been a favourite place for Jesus to find peace and quiet, away from the hustle and bustle of Jerusalem. It was here that he took his disciples late on the Thursday night after the Passover meal had finished. Jesus clearly needed time alone with God, but he also wanted his friends nearby as he faced the biggest decision of his life – a decision that would mean life or death for the whole world.

Christians believe that Jesus was not only God but also fully human, which means that Jesus felt fear and was open to temptation just like any of us. It would have been so simple just to turn his back on the suffering that lay ahead, which he calls 'the cup' he must drink. No wonder he wrestled with God. His friends must have heard his sighs and groans, but it was late and they were very tired. They couldn't stay awake to be with him, as he'd asked them to. It was already beginning to happen: even his own disciples were letting him down and he would have to face what was coming on his own. But this decision in this garden was the only way to repair the damage of that other decision in the garden of Eden long ago, when Adam and Eve gave in to the temptation to follow their way and not God's.

⁇ Questions

- ▶ Why did Jesus choose to come to Gethsemane to pray rather than stay in the upstairs room in Jerusalem?
- ▶ What big decisions have you had to make, and what helped you to make them?
- ▶ Why was it important that Jesus would die on a cross?
- ▶ How could his closest disciples let him down in the way that they did?

Visual aid

Gethsemane was a place where olives grew. Have a few olives to taste.

Activity idea

Have you ever been out in the garden or in the open, late at night? Choose an evening to do this together. Notice how different it feels to be outdoors in the dark and listen to the sounds. Now that you are outside, is there anything that helps you to think about God or encourages you to pray? Imagine the tired disciples waiting in the dark and trying to stay awake for Jesus.

Prayer idea

It is from this story that Christians get the idea of kneeling for prayer, just as Jesus did. Traditionally Jews would stand with hands raised when they prayed, so why did Jesus do it differently here? For your prayers today, experiment with a new way of standing, sitting or kneeling, and perhaps also change what you do with your hands. Whatever you pray about, pray the prayer three times with spaces in between, just as Jesus did in the story.

Old Testament story link

This is the story of how Moses went to pray on a hilltop with help from his friends, while the Israelites were fighting a battle down below.
EXODUS 17:8–15

Key verse

'My Father, if it is not possible for this cup to be taken away unless I drink it, may your will be done.'
MATTHEW 26:42

6 Peter denies Jesus

[57] Those who had arrested Jesus took him to Caiaphas the high priest, where the teachers of the law and the elders had assembled. [58] But Peter followed him at a distance, right up to the courtyard of the high priest. He entered and sat down with the guards to see the outcome…

[69] Now Peter was sitting out in the courtyard, and a servant-girl came to him. 'You also were with Jesus of Galilee,' she said.

[70] But he denied it before them all. 'I don't know what you're talking about,' he said.

[71] Then he went out to the gateway, where another servant-girl saw him and said to the people there, 'This fellow was with Jesus of Nazareth.'

[72] He denied it again, with an oath: 'I don't know the man!'

[73] After a little while, those standing there went up to Peter and said, 'Surely you are one of them; your accent gives you away.'

[74] Then he began to call down curses, and he swore to them, 'I don't know the man!'

Immediately a cock crowed. [75] Then Peter remembered the word Jesus had spoken: 'Before the cock crows, you will disown me three times.' And he went outside and wept bitterly.

MATTHEW 26:57–58, 69–75

Commentary

Jesus had been arrested in the garden of Gethsemane and taken to the high priest's house for trial in the middle of the night. The religious leaders were anxious to get rid of him as soon as possible. The disciples had all run away when Jesus was captured, except for Peter, who followed the temple guards secretly and made his way to where Jesus was being held. Inside they were busy interrogating Jesus, accusing him of all sorts of things that he hadn't done. Jesus said very little, but just once he let them know that he was from God, and this caused uproar.

Peter was nearby in the courtyard and possibly heard the angry shouts, but was helpless to do anything. He must have been terrified and, as a result, he denied being one of Jesus' followers, even saying that he never knew him. Jesus had warned him that this would happen, but Peter hadn't believed it. No wonder he burst into tears and disappeared off into the darkness.

This is a remarkable piece of honest reporting. Peter went on to become a leader of the church, but he didn't mind people knowing how low he had once sunk. Perhaps he wanted them to understand how much Jesus loved him and, therefore, each one of us, that he could forgive even this betrayal.

?? Questions

▶ Was Peter brave or foolish to follow Jesus to the courtyard?

▶ Have you ever let someone down? How did you feel?

▶ Have you ever been let down by someone else? Were you able to forgive them?

▶ What was it that made Peter betray his best friend like this?

19

 ## Visual aid

Find a picture of a cockerel and have a go at adding your own sound effects to the story. This sound must have been a permanent reminder to Peter of what happened that night.

 ## Activity idea

Peter was put under pressure to reply quickly to the people's questions. So much must have been going on his head: should he say 'yes' to knowing Jesus or deny all knowledge of him? Between you, try to imagine the quarrel going on inside his own mind before he spoke. What arguments are there for saying one thing or the other? What were the risks involved? What was his head saying as opposed to his heart? Try to step into Peter's conscience and explore the story from this point of view.

 ## Prayer idea

After a short time of quiet, ask God to forgive you for the ways you have let him down and then be honest with each other and forgive each other for the ways you have let each other down. Sometimes, as for Peter, tears are involved when we say 'sorry' properly like this.

 ## Old Testament story link

David was Israel's most famous king. This is his prayer, saying 'sorry' after he had let God down very badly.
PSALM 51:1-19

Key verse
And Peter went outside and wept bitterly.
MATTHEW 26:75

7 The death sentence

¹⁵ Now it was the governor's custom at the festival to release a prisoner chosen by the crowd. ¹⁶ At that time they had a well-known prisoner whose name was Jesus Barabbas. ¹⁷ So when the crowd had gathered, Pilate asked them, 'Which one do you want me to release to you: Jesus Barabbas, or Jesus who is called the Messiah?' ¹⁸ For he knew it was out of self-interest that they had handed Jesus over to him…

²⁰ But the chief priests and the elders persuaded the crowd to ask for Barabbas and to have Jesus executed.

²¹ 'Which of the two do you want me to release to you?' asked the governor.

'Barabbas,' they answered.

²² 'What shall I do, then, with Jesus who is called the Messiah?' Pilate asked.

They all answered, 'Crucify him!'

²³ 'Why? What crime has he committed?' asked Pilate.

But they shouted all the louder, 'Crucify him!'

²⁴ When Pilate saw that he was getting nowhere, but that instead an uproar was starting, he took water and washed his hands in front of the crowd. 'I am innocent of this man's blood,' he said. 'It is your responsibility!'

²⁵ All the people answered, 'His blood is on us and on our children!'

²⁶ Then he released Barabbas to them. But he had Jesus flogged, and handed him over to be crucified.

MATTHEW 27:15–18, 20–26

Commentary

The tragic events of Good Friday are rapidly moving to a conclusion. The trial in the early morning resulted in a verdict of 'guilty', but, because the Romans held power in Judea, the religious leaders had to ask the Roman governor to approve Jesus' death sentence. Pontius Pilate interrogated Jesus but could find no reason to condemn him, so he thought he would appeal to the crowds, using the local custom of setting a prisoner free at Passover time. Barabbas was someone who had tried to get rid of the Romans by force, but he had been captured. He had tried to be the sort of revolutionary king the people wanted, and that many had hoped Jesus would become. So who would the crowd choose? The chief priests and leaders left nothing to chance and stirred up the people to call for Barabbas.

It's hard to believe that so many who must have heard Jesus speak, or, at the very least, heard of the miracles he had done, now turn against him. It seems that people in a crowd often act against their better judgement. Pilate can't find any fault in Jesus. The truth is that only through the willing death of someone who had done nothing wrong could the power of evil be broken.

?? Questions

▶ What impression of Pilate's character do you get from the story?

▶ What do you think Barabbas thought about Jesus and what happened that day?

▶ Have you ever gone along with what everyone is saying even when you didn't agree?

▶ How does this story make you feel?

Visual aid

Make a bowl of water, some soap and a towel available. Give everybody the opportunity to wash their hands. Pilate washed his hands as a way of letting the people know that, whatever happened next, it was not his responsibility – but does this really let him off the hook?

 # Activity idea

From the internet find a picture depicting the moment when Pilate presented Jesus to the crowd. There is a famous one by the artist Antonio Ciseri, called *Behold the Man!* Talk about the different people you can see in the picture and imagine what each one is thinking at that moment. What do you think is going through Jesus' mind as the crowds call for his death?

 # Prayer idea

Barabbas is a murderer, the leaders are jealous, Pilate blames the crowd and the crowds are swayed by the feelings of the moment; only Jesus is innocent. On a blank outline of a cross, use different dark colours to scribble inside the outline until the cross is all coloured in. Each scribble represents some of the bad things that Jesus is going to battle with on the cross, such as the hatred and hurt, betrayal and anger that are all represented in this story.

 # Old Testament story link

Long ago, the prophet Isaiah wrote about someone who would suffer on behalf of others to take away what was wrong.
ISAIAH 52:13—53:10

Key verse
'Why? What crime has he committed?' asked Pilate.
MATTHEW 27:23

8 The road to the cross

[26] As the soldiers led him away, they seized Simon from Cyrene, who was on his way in from the country, and put the cross on him and made him carry it behind Jesus. [27] A large number of people followed him, including women who mourned and wailed for him. [28] Jesus turned and said to them, 'Daughters of Jerusalem, do not weep for me; weep for yourselves and for your children. [29] For the time will come when you will say, "Blessed are the childless women, the wombs that never bore and the breasts that never nursed!" [30] Then "they will say to the mountains, 'Fall on us!' and to the hills, 'Cover us!'" [31] For if people do these things when the tree is green, what will happen when it is dry?'

[32] Two other men, both criminals, were also led out with him to be executed. [33] When they came to the place called the Skull, they crucified him there, along with the criminals – one on his right, the other on his left. [34] Jesus said, 'Father, forgive them, for they do not know what they are doing.' And they divided up his clothes by casting lots.

[35] The people stood watching, and the rulers even sneered at him. They said, 'He saved others; let him save himself if he is God's Messiah, the Chosen One.'

While the crowd stood there watching Jesus, the soldiers gambled for his clothes. The leaders insulted him by saying, 'He saved others. Now he should save himself, if he really is God's chosen Messiah!'

[36] The soldiers also came up and mocked him. They offered him wine vinegar [37] and said, 'If you are the king of the Jews, save yourself.'

LUKE 23:26–37

Commentary

To die as a criminal on a cross was a terrible punishment, designed to act as a deterrent to those who were thinking of breaking the law. It was public, cruel and humiliating. The criminals had to carry a heavy crosspiece of wood to the place where they would be executed so that everyone could see them on their journey through the streets. Jesus and two others had to carry their own crosses in this way, but it was too much for Jesus, who was weak from all the beatings he had received, and a passerby was ordered to carry the wooden beam instead. Jesus had some sad words to say to the women who were crying. He seems to be predicting the day when even more terrible things would happen to people in Jerusalem as the result of war.

The place where the crosses were set up was known as 'The Skull'. Perhaps the rocks there looked like a human skull, or maybe it was just because it was the place where so many had died. Jesus was nailed to the cross. He was laughed at by the crowds and insulted by the soldiers. It is the most horrible climax of evil that you can imagine, but right at the heart of all this darkness come Jesus' words of forgiveness. The worst that could be done to him has happened, but it has not broken him, because God's love is still alive inside him. This love will soon show itself stronger than death itself.

?? Questions

▶ What do you think Simon told his family about what had happened that day?

▶ What did Jesus mean by his words to the women?

▶ What, for you, is the worst part of this story?

▶ How did the leaders insult Jesus?

Visual aid

A simple cross is the focus you need for today's story. You will also need some small stones for the activity below.

 # Activity idea

Jesus once talked about 'taking up your cross' as a way of describing what it meant to follow him. In fact, anyone who literally did this was on their way to execution. Jesus was asking people to put all that was bad to death if they wanted to be his disciples. Next to the simple cross, build up a large pile of stones to represent all the bad things you can think of in this world today – things like murder, violence, lying, abuse and hatred. When you have finished, rearrange the stones to spell the letters of the word 'forgiven'.

 # Prayer idea

On a large piece of paper, draw several big teardrops to represent the suffering of the world and then, as a prayer, draw a cross inside each of the teardrops. Below all of this, write the words, 'God understands because Jesus suffered on the cross.'

 # Old Testament story link

Zechariah had a vision of a man called Joshua, who had all his dirty clothes taken away. Later he writes that this is a picture of guilt being taken away in one single day.
ZECHARIAH 3:1–10

Key verse
Jesus said, 'Father, forgive them.'
LUKE 23:34

9 The crucifixion

³⁸ There was a written notice above him, which read: THIS IS THE KING OF THE JEWS.

³⁹ One of the criminals who hung there hurled insults at him: 'Aren't you the Messiah? Save yourself and us!'

⁴⁰ But the other criminal rebuked him. 'Don't you fear God,' he said, 'since you are under the same sentence? ⁴¹ We are punished justly, for we are getting what our deeds deserve. But this man has done nothing wrong.'

⁴² Then he said, 'Jesus, remember me when you come into your kingdom.'

⁴³ Jesus answered him, 'Truly I tell you, today you will be with me in paradise.'

⁴⁴ It was now about noon, and darkness came over the whole land until three in the afternoon, ⁴⁵ for the sun stopped shining. And the curtain of the temple was torn in two. ⁴⁶ Jesus called out with a loud voice, 'Father, into your hands I commit my spirit.' When he had said this, he breathed his last.

⁴⁷ The centurion, seeing what had happened, praised God and said, 'Surely this was a righteous man.' ⁴⁸ When all the people who had gathered to witness this sight saw what took place, they beat their breasts and went away. ⁴⁹ But all those who knew him, including the women who had

💬 Commentary

Even when he was hanging from the cross, Jesus continued to show love and bring hope to others. The criminals on either side of him were going through the same agony, but, unlike Jesus, they had committed crimes and deserved to be punished. One joins in with the crowd's insults. The other is clearly sorry for what he has done and simply hopes to be part of God's kingdom when he dies. Jesus promises that this criminal will be with him in paradise that day.

By now it is afternoon and the end is near. It is almost as if the whole world goes dark, but it is also the moment when Jesus defeats the powers of darkness. The curtain in the innermost part of the temple, where the high priest used to go and meet with God once a year, is torn apart, and the way to God is now open because of what Jesus has done. Only a completely innocent man could have achieved this; even the Roman soldier agrees that Jesus has done no wrong.

The crowd and Jesus' friends saw only defeat and went away broken-hearted, but in fact what had happened that day was the greatest miracle Jesus had ever done.

?? Questions

▶ The two criminals had quite different attitudes towards Jesus. What could explain this, do you think?

▶ Why do you think it went so dark that afternoon?

▶ The officer on guard duty had probably only just met Jesus, so what made him think that Jesus was such a good man?

▶ Can you imagine what was going on in the minds of Jesus' close friends and the women who were watching at a distance?

Visual aid

Find an old piece of fabric that will tear easily from top to bottom. Drape it over a board showing the word 'heaven', and then pull it away to reveal what is hidden behind it.

 # Activity idea

Talk about what it would have been like to witness all these things. Strangely, Christians call this day Good Friday. Talk about why they call it 'good'. Now take the letters of the phrase 'Jesus dies' and rearrange them to read 'Jesus' side'. Because of his death we can all come close to God.

 # Prayer idea

Anyone can get to heaven because of Jesus. The second criminal discovered this to be true. Offer a special prayer – either out loud or quietly – to say that you will trust Jesus just as the thief on the cross did. Heaven starts right here and now for everyone who prays this sort of prayer.

 # Old Testament story link

Many people believe that Jesus was remembering this psalm as he hung on the cross.
PSALM 22

Key verse
Jesus answered him, 'Truly I tell you, today you will be with me in paradise.'
LUKE 23:43

10 The empty tomb

[11] Now Mary stood outside the tomb crying. As she wept, she bent over to look into the tomb [12] and saw two angels in white, seated where Jesus' body had been, one at the head and the other at the foot.

[13] They asked her, 'Woman, why are you crying?'

'They have taken my Lord away,' she said, 'and I don't know where they have put him.' [14] At this, she turned round and saw Jesus standing there, but she did not realise that it was Jesus.

[15] He asked her, 'Woman, why are you crying? Who is it you are looking for?'

Thinking he was the gardener, she said, 'Sir, if you have carried him away, tell me where you have put him, and I will get him.'

[16] Jesus said to her, 'Mary.'

She turned towards him and cried out in Aramaic, 'Rabboni!' (which means 'Teacher').

[17] Jesus said, 'Do not hold on to me, for I have not yet ascended to the Father. Go instead to my brothers and tell them, "I am ascending to my Father and your Father, to my God and your God."'

[18] Mary Magdalene went to the disciples with the news: 'I have seen the Lord!' And she told them that he had said these things to her.

JOHN 20:11–18

Commentary

Jesus' dead body had been hastily taken down from the cross just before sunset on the Friday. A Jewish leader who was a secret disciple offered his own rock tomb nearby for the burial, and a stone was rolled over the entrance. The women, including Mary Magdalene, had watched all this. The next day was a special Jewish sabbath, so no one travelled anywhere.

It wasn't until early on the Sunday morning that Mary could go to the tomb to pay her last respects. To her surprise, the stone had been rolled away. She ran to fetch Peter and John, who came to see for themselves what had happened. After they left, Mary was alone in the garden in tears, trying to make sense of what had happened. This is when she saw the angels, and then heard a voice asking her why she was crying.

Clearly Jesus looked different from before. Her last sight of him had been of a terribly disfigured body on a cross, and perhaps that is why she did not recognise him at first. Only when he said her name did she realise that this was really Jesus, back from the dead. Mary longed to hold on to him, but Jesus wanted her to learn not to cling to his earthly body any more, but to trust him as a spiritual presence, just as everyone else would do who came to believe in Jesus later.

?? Questions

▶ How did Mary imagine she would be able to roll the stone back from the tomb?

▶ Why didn't Mary recognise Jesus at first?

▶ What did Mary fear might have happened to Jesus' body?

▶ What helped Mary to recognise that it was Jesus?

▶ Why didn't Jesus allow Mary to touch him?

Visual aid

Look at some pictures from the internet of people's ideas about the resurrection of Jesus. Many artists have found it hard to portray this moment. Perhaps a simple abstract painting of blinding light is the best that can be achieved.

 ## Activity idea

Use some craft materials (possibly air-drying clay) to create a cave with an entrance over which you place a round stone. Alternatively, create a tomb and entrance from some of the furniture and blankets that you can find around the home. Inside the cave place some cloths, piled neatly like the grave clothes that Jesus left behind.

 ## Prayer idea

A traditional greeting between Christians on Easter Day is 'Christ is risen', to which the reply is 'He is risen indeed. Hallelujah.' Use this as a family at the end of each prayer you make today. Your prayers could perhaps be focused on those who are sad because someone has died, those who are frightened about the future and those who tell others that Jesus is risen from the dead.

 ## Old Testament story link

This is part of the song of victory that Moses and the people sang after they had escaped from Egypt through the Red Sea.
EXODUS 15:11-18

Key verse
'Tell them, "I am ascending to my Father and your Father, to my God and your God."'
JOHN 20:17

The Bible Reading Fellowship
15 The Chambers, Vineyard
Abingdon OX14 3FE
brf.org.uk

The Bible Reading Fellowship (BRF) is a Registered Charity (233280)

ISBN 978 1 80039 101 7
First published 2021
10 9 8 7 6 5 4 3 2 1 0
All rights reserved

Acknowledgements
Scripture quotations taken from The Holy Bible, New International Version Anglicised.
Copyright © 1979, 1984, 2011 Biblica. Used by permission of Hodder & Stoughton Ltd,
an Hachette UK company. All rights reserved. 'NIV' is a registered trademark of Biblica
UK trademark number 1448790.

Every effort has been made to trace and contact copyright owners for material used
in this resource. We apologise for any inadvertent omissions or errors, and would ask
those concerned to contact us so that full acknowledgement can be made in the future.

A catalogue record for this book is available from the British Library

Printed and bound in the UK by Zenith Media NP4 0DQ